St. Francis

OF ASSISI

The Poverello

BY MARK HEGENER

THE POVERELLO: St. Francis of Assisi by Mark
Hegener, OFM. Copyright © 1956 and 1989,
Franciscan Herald Press, 1434 West 51st Street,
Chicago, Illinois 60609. All rights reserved.

Eighth printing, 1989

Franciscan Herald Press
1434 West 51st Street
Chicago, Illinois 60609

The Poverello

St. Francis
OF ASSISI

FOREWORD

There is a kind of pitying pathos in the nickname which the Italians gave St. Francis even in his own lifetime. They called him "Il Poverello"—the poor little fellow.

But the undertones of the name indicate not pity for the man because he was poor, but admiration because he was rich. The Church goes on to state it quite frankly in the versicle sung each year when the death of St. Francis is commemorated on his feast day, October 4. Gathered together, the friars sing: "Poor and humble St. Francis enters Heaven laden with riches." To enter Heaven laden with riches is such a jolting paradox to the little, humble poor man people saw here on earth!

And St. Francis is still a stark lesson to our times when success is measured by money, and power the yardstick for greatness. It is still the rule for entrance into the Kingdom that we *become as little children;* the law remains unaltered that the *poor in spirit* shall inherit the land of Heaven.

Poor and little. Il Poverello! That was how St. Francis thought of himself too. His friars, he said, were to be a new race of people which the Heavenly Father gave to his beloved Son; they were to be unlike all others in *poverty* and *humility* (littleness) and were to be content to have Christ only!

Across the centuries men have rushed to meet this little poor fellow. He inspires. He is dynamic. You cannot meet him without being changed. And when he clasps your hand he leaves an impression—and it may be a grace-bearing stain from his sacred stigmata that will stay with you always! With his handclasp he imparts his greeting: "The Lord give you peace!" And the impression he leaves is filled with peace and blessing — the very slogan of his Order. Pax et Bonum!

Mark Hegener

New life was sweeping through Italy in 1182 when Francis of Assisi was born. From the wandering troubadours and jongleurs came tales of bravery and romance that set the young blood of youth racing. Crusaders coming back from the East during the past century had opened up wide vistas never dreamed of before; there were new lands, new riches, new beauties. Especially new fabrics. Staggering was the glimpse which the future held in store.

The city states, proud of new power, flexed their muscles. New-rich merchants, hardly a generation removed from serfdom, gingerly challenged the power of nobility with the sound ring of coin. The Church itself was about to pit her full force against the might of the Hohenstaufens threatening to sweep through Italy to possess the two Sicilies.

From the serf and his liege lord up through knight, baron, emperor and pope, tempers were taunt and tensions ready to be released. Thus the world went on plodding its hard road of conflict, while the storms of history drove the devout to yearn with all their heart for the peace that is not of this world.

"Pax et Bonum — Peace and Welfare", was the promise extended by a stranger wandering through Assisi's streets when a son was born to Peter Bernardone and Donna Pica in 1182. The pilgrim rapped at their door and asked to see the boy.

Bernardone was away in France on business but the mother had the child baptized John. When his father came home, in his love for France he called the boy Francesco; perhaps too in deference to Donna Pica, who seems to have come from Picardy. To this small French heritage Francis clung. Often in moments of exceptional elation he spoke in French.

Though the Bernardone family was not of the nobility, still it could hold up its head with the best of Assisi. No longer was blue blood the differentiating principle between classes. It was money. And Peter Bernardone had acquired a goodly share of money through a brisk dry goods business. New fabrics and dyes from the East brought good money from those who wished to splash about bold heraldic colors. Men could finally be their own masters now. No longer was it necessary to "belong" to a feudal lord for protection. Artisans and craftsmen and merchants became independent, built cities and made them strong. Bernardone was such an independent man. He had finally made it on his own.

BERNARDONE'S SON

Francis makes an abrupt appearance on the stage of history. Suddenly Assisi is aware of a young man with life and verve, venturesome and valiant. Peter Bernardone was willing to give his son anything — all the things he himself did not have as a boy. The new-rich are the same the world over. So Francis grew up. A pleasant boy, vivacious yet never bold, perceptive but no pansy, sensitive to values yet hankering after the proverbial youthful joy of living. And "live it" he did. The crowd of young men he led about dubbed him the King of Youth. The dean of teens.

Through it all Francis was pure in mind and heart, possessing those endearing qualities that made him genial, gentle, joyful, generous, chivalrous, daring, and original. Though small in frame, in his heart leaped a flame of indomitable energy.

He was a young man very much like all the other young men — only more so. Being a boy in fairly easy circumstances, he grew up in an atmosphere of money-making and romance. Both forces left their imprint on Francis: one attracted and one repulsed. Money-making as a rule starves out romance; but the reverse happened to Francis.

One of his earliest ambitions was to be a soldier — to fight for a cause. A knight-errant! In the songs of chivalry he heard tell of these knights. Every young man heard and learned the songs by heart. Sang them and dreamed dreams. Francis sang the songs of the troubadours in French.

These songs remained with him all his life and the ideal of chivalry colored his whole future outlook. "My Knights of the Round Table" he called

his friars. "We are minstrels of the Lord," he told them, "and our job is to gladden the hearts of people." Charlemagne, Roland and Oliver and all the paladins were among his heroes.

But the perfect knight must have a lady for whose sake he will gladly make sacrifice and lay down his life. Within the poetic tradition of the troubadours, this lady could be an idea, spiritualized and etherealized by the poet-lovers' imagination. Who should be the lady of Francis and what form should his chivalrous devotion take?

PRISONER OF WAR

Francis soon had an opportunity to be a soldier and fulfill part of his dream. The local nobility of Assisi had allied themselves with the ruling puppet of the Emperor. When the mob of Assisi stormed the citadel (to this day a ruins called La Rocca) of the count of Spoleto, the nobility of Assisi allied themselves with the neighboring town of Perugia.

At St. John's bridge, between the two cities, the military forces of Assisi were defeated. Among the prisoners led away up to Perugia was also Francis. The year, 1202. The victors put Francis among the captive knights, and when his high spirits roused the resentment of his fellow prisoners, he replied to one of his critics with full assurance of future fame: "They are going to honor me all over the world some day." One of the embittered knights found his sole comfort in Francis' kindness.

Released from prison after a year, Francis came home weak and wondering if he had seen himself and the world correctly at all. Ill health filled him with sadness for the first time in his life. Convalescing from his illness, he strolled, cane in hand, beyond the city walls. But he no longer felt the teenage thrill at the sight of the broad, shimmering valley and the vineyards. Depressed and uneasy, Francis looked for a solvent for his heavy heartedness.

He was restive, rearing, anxious. A gnawing yearning pulled him from one idea to another. Now and then his gay companions and jolly parties broke the spell of melancholy. Now, too, for the first time he became *aware* of poverty — the first faint glimpse of Lady Poverty — when he accosted a beggar in the street. Francis cheerfully gave him an alms.

One day, though, while busy in his father's shop with his bolts of cloth, he turned a beggar away with a little irritation. At once he reconsidered: "If he had pleaded in the name of some count or baron, you would surely have complied with his request." Yet, had not the beggar asked for an alms in the Name of Christ, the hidden King of the Universe, who wishes to be fed in the hungry and sheltered in the homeless?

THE GLORY ROAD

Suddenly Francis' spiritual crisis seemed resolved. An opportunity for name, fame and fortune seemed at hand. The forces of the Emperor Frederick II

and of Pope Innocent III were at war over the mastery of Sicily. Down in Apulia the pope's general, Walter of Brienne, was battling the Hohenstaufen general, Markward of Anweiler. When an Assisi nobleman made ready to join Walter of Brienne's army. Francis seized the opportunity, hoping that he might win the spurs of knighthood on the field of battle.

He dressed in extravagantly expensive equipment. Shortly before they set out, he met a poverty-stricken knight, gave the poor man all the equipment he had prepared for the campaign, and headed for Spoleto.

Bivouacked on the way to Apulia, Francis had a dream of a beautiful castle heavily stocked with flashing military shields, lances, saddlery. In admiration he asked for whom all that military splendor was intended, and learned that it was for him and his men-at-arms. With a head full of knightly ambitions, this was fuel to his desires. "Now I know I am going to be a great prince," he cried full of joy on awakening.

The raw recruits of Italy's finest manhood for Walter of Brienne's army gathered at Spoleto. In a half-sleep, a voice asked Francis where he was going in such a hurry. "Francis," the voice insisted, "who can do more for you, the lord or the vassal, a man of wealth or a poor man?" "The lord," returned Francis. "Then why are you leaving the lord for the vassal, the wealthy man for a poor man?"

It took but an instant. But those words made an instant and irrevocable change in Francis. The dream that he had been seeking was beginning to take on reality. Back of the seeming power of mortals he was to recognize the power of the Lord: back of the seeming splendor of the world, the splendor of the kingdom of God. From now on this new insight was to be the principle of life and the rigid guides for living. "What would you have me do, Lord?" he asked. "Go back home and it shall be told you what you are to do."

Dazed, he returns to Assisi with the courage to appear a coward. How live that down?

THE KNIGHT'S LADY

It would almost seem that Francis backslid very quickly from the high resolve at Spoleto. He still leads the revels, but not with the old zest. He was shaken, bruised and confused, lacking in energy, like a man in ccnflict, drained of vitality. The valley, the mountains, the sky seemed empty again; the joy of earlier dreams withered.

Somewhere about this time he encountered a leper while riding outside of Assisi. The sight and smell of lepers filled him with unutterable loathing. "As he used to say," says Celano, his earliest biographer, "the sight of lepers was so bitter to him that when in the days of his vanity he looked at their houses about two miles off, he held his nose. . . . One day, while still in the habit of the world, he met a leper and, overcoming himself, went near and kissed him." The act was a victory which Francis never forgot.

From the black corners of Assisi the poor loomed up large to cast long shadows before him in the light of the new faith rising in Francis' heart. And Francis began to dream about his Lady.

Sometimes he is abstracted in the midst of the revels. Suddenly the thought of the poor Christ and his poor little Mother stunned Francis still in his tracks. He was lagging behind the rest of the revellers. To them he seemed like a man in love. "Francis, are you going to get married?" they asked. In the pressure of the moment his decision was crystallized and he answered: "I *am* going to marry a bride, one nobler and fairer than any you have ever seen, one that will be outstanding for beauty and will impress everybody else for wit."

The Bride he was thinking of was the Lady despised of all others, whose praises he sang and whose champion he became for the rest of his life—the Lady Poverty. There was no lady of romance who could demand greater sacrifices. It was a kind of inverted chivalry!

The spiritual knighthood, with Christ the liege lord and Lady Poverty his bride, began to take shape. Following Christ, Francis saw, would mean a complete self-stripping, as the Son of God had stripped himself of his Godhead, even of respectable manhood, to die an outcast and a criminal—divested of clothes, peeled of the last shred of respectability, even his good name.

THE FINAL STRUGGLE

But poverty was loathsome to Francis. His sensitive soul crept at the idea of a life stripped of finery and security. To gain strength he made a pilgrimage to Rome. He went straight to St. Peters, up the nave to the Confessio before St. Peter's tomb. Francis knelt at the grating and looked down the shaft. Visitors flung in small offerings. Disappointed at the niggardly amounts the pilgrims were giving to St. Peter, Francis threw all he had into the shaft with one generous gesture.

He left the church and suddenly noticed the beggars clutching the sleeves of those who approached the doors and whining, "Un soldo, signore . . . per amor di Dio . . ." For the love of God: that was what the beggar had said to him in his father's shop. Could he stand being that poor? In a dramatic decision he exchanged his tailored clothes for the rags of a beggar and panhandled for alms in front of St. Peter's.

Back in Assisi he continued his reflections, waiting in solitude for the voice at Spoleto which had promised to tell him what to do. At last in the half-

ruined little Church of San Damiano outside the walls of Assisi the voice spoke to him. From the old Byzantine crucifix the wide-open eyes of our Savior were fixed on Francis: "Francis," said our Lord, "do you not see how my house is going to ruin? Then go and build it up again!" Trembling, Francis replied, "I will be glad to do so, Lord."

At last, the voice! At last, an objective! Finally, he knew what he must do.

IN CHRIST'S SERVICE

Losing all perspective for a moment, Francis could think of nothing but the immediate repair of tumbled-down San Damiano. Where get the funds? Chesterton puts it with brutal frankness: "he stole." He stole a bale of goods from the warehouse, loaded it on a horse, rode to the Foligno market and sold horse, cloth and all. Francis was about 25 or 26 years old. The result of this episode was a breach with his father.

The poor little priest in charge of San Damiano would not take the money, fearing the wealthy Peter Bernardone. But he did allow Peter's son to live with him in his dingy dwelling next to the crumbling church. Francis tossed the money on a window sill, for to him money had no further value than to serve a holy purpose.

Bernardone ordered Francis hunted up. The young man fled to a cavern, shaken and afraid. But in the cave, with prayer, he gained a new kind of courage. Finally firm in his resolution with a clear mind as to what he must do, he came out of the cave and walked into the city of Assisi, emaciated and ragged but with fixed focus.

Once held up as the greatest young man in Assisi, the most promising, the most eligible — now the children ridiculed him as a fool. Stones, mud, sticks came flying at him. Amidst all the rowdyism, Peter Bernardone flailed his way through the crowd, dragged his son home and locked him in a cellar jail. Later, with Bernardone away on a journey, Donna Pica set Francis free. But the break which had long since taken place at heart, was bound to come before the eyes of everybody.

Peter Bernardone brought suit against his son for the goods taken from the house—first before the city authorities and then before the bishop, because following his conversion, Francis recognized none but the bishop's jurisdiction over him.

In the court of Bishop Guido of Assisi Francis brought the money back—it had lain all this while in the church window. Certainly, thought the bishop, Francis will enter a religious order now. Suddenly Francis stood up, gave back to his father not only the money but all his clothing as well, stripping himself right down to a hair shirt. Standing in the midst of the court he made his declaration of utter dependence on the fatherly providence of God: "From now on I will say, Our Father who are in Heaven; it shall be no longer, Father Peter Bernardone."

The final struggle was ended and for Francis it meant a paradoxical reversal of all the world's values. He had made the first reverse in the court

of the bishop. The others were to come. Poverty comes to be real riches, to beg is "a great nobility and dignity." Honor becomes shame. "Perfect joy" is achieved by accepting willingly and suffering gladly all the miseries and discomforts of life; simplicity is wisdom; to rule is to serve. In giving we receive. In pardoning we are pardoned.

THE NEW LIFE

Bishop Guido covered Francis' nakedness with his mantle and gave him a rough peasant's tunic to wear. St. Bonaventure records an important detail. Before he put it on he drew a great cross on the tunic with chalk. He was a crusader! Francis left the bishop's court singing. Up in the mountains, robbers challenged him, "Who are you?" Immediately Francis answered, "I am the herald of the great King!" A snow bath was the reward for this dramatic declaration.

At the Benedictine convent on Mt. Subasio he worked as a skullery boy for a few months, then went on to Gubbio. Finally back in Assisi, he began a strenuous and active life, divided between care of the lepers, hard manual labor, and begging. At the end of his life he begins his Testament with the words:

"The Lord gave me, Brother Francis, the grace of beginning to do penance in this way: that, when I was in sin, it seemed extremely bitter to me to look at lepers, and the Lord himself led me in among them and I practiced mercy with them. And when ʾ came away from them, what seemed bitter to me, was changed to sweetness of spirit and body for me" *Words,* no. 282.

He restored three churches near Assisi, among them San Damiano and the Porticuncula, with his own hands, and the help of any volunteers he could collect. He begged for the lepers, he begged materials for the churches, he begged food and clothing for himself, when the odd jobs he did failed to supply them. It was a trial to beg from the people in Assisi with whom he had associated before. The gay youth they had known shows up a beggar asking for whatever mixed victuals they wished to give. And mixed they must have been! In begging for his food, as when he begged for the first time in front of St. Peter's in Rome, he broke out into French song—the language of chivalry. The biography of

the Three Companions tells us that he begged in French "because he loved to speak the French tongue, albeit he spoke it not aright."

The lepers remained his special care. And it can be truly said that he changed a whole society's attitude toward that knotty medieval problem. The only cure men knew for leprosy was ostracisim from society. These abandoned hulks of humanity were certainly the least of Christ's brethren. With them Francis began; in them he saw Christ. Tending the lepers was one of the first tasks he imposed on new recruits to his order, besides enjoining on his friars manual labor and begging. He had practiced all three himself.

DAY OF DECISION

February 24, 1209, the feast of St. Matthias, was decisive in Francis' life. So was the place—the little chapel of the Portiuncula, the "little portion," or

St. Mary of the Angels, said to have been erected very long ago by pilgrims returning from the Holy Land. The angels, so the story was passed on, loved the spot and had now and then appeared to people there. Francis had rebuilt the crumbling walls in honor of the Blessed Virgin. Today it is venerated as the Mother Church of the whole Franciscan Order.

Now he was assisting at Mass and listened to the Gospel being read in the rebuilt church. Our Lord is charging the Apostles (Mt. 10, 9 - 13): " . . . Do not keep gold or silver or money in your belts, nor wallet for your journey, nor two tunics, nor sandals, nor staff . . ." After Mass he asked the priest to explain the passage. The priest interpreted the words. On the spot Francis put away wallet, staff, tooled leather belt and shoes he had been wearing as a hermit. "This is what I want," he cried, "this is what I am looking for, this is what I desire with my whole heart."

For his leather belt he substituted a rope and the Franciscan habit was complete.

Now the Lord was asking more of him. In addition to the charge to rebuild the church given to him from the crucifix at San Damiano, he was receiving the commission to go out and declare that the kingdom of Heaven was near. Careful to find out just how he must begin, he was told: "When you enter a house, offer them this greeting and say, Peace be to this house."

No longer a hermit, Francis became again a leader of men, leading his knights on their great adventure of liberating the world from the enemy giants of avarice and lust and hatred and pride. The glory and the sacrifices made for peace he made as compelling and romantic as the glory and the sacrifices men made for war!

FIRST FOLLOWERS

It was more than two years since Francis left the court of Bishop Guido. Now he began to appear in the public squares of Assisi and preach the word of God. He began with the blessing, "The Lord give you peace." What he said was plain and forceful, filled with the fire of a man fearfully in love. He liked to relate a parable in plain words. When he no longer felt the spirit stirring him, he quit speaking. The inexhaustible enthusiasm of a mission, of assurance, of truth, beamed from his face.

It must have surprised Francis to have his first preaching meet with such enthusiasm. But this was something new to the people. Sermons were never before preached on city streets, but in the great churches and most of the time in the Latin language which few could understand.

The first person to follow him was a man "of pious, plain turn of mind," merchant Bernard of Quintavalle. He had observed Francis for some time, studied him carefully and decided to find out for himself whether this young man was saint or charlatan. He invited Francis to his home. That night the merchant asked his guest for advice. He was troubled. "If a man has had more or less property from his master and kept it for many years," he said, "but now does not wish to keep it any longer, what is the more proper thing for him to do with it?" Francis replied that the man should give the property back to the giver. Bernard evidently expected that answer: he put all his temporal goods in Francis' hands. Later they disposed of them in the city square.

Before venturing to dispose of Bernard's goods, they resolved to go to St. Nicholas church and ask God just how it must be done. Peter Cattani, the pious attorney of the chapter of St. Rufinus cathedral, joined them on the way.

Francis decided to use the medieval method of solving a difficult problem: it was a method based on faith that God would guide aright the opening of the Missal. He prayed, approached the altar and opened the Holy Book. Kneeling, he opened it and read the words: "If you wish to be perfect, go, sell all you have and give it to the poor, and you shall have a treasure in Heaven."

A second time he opened the book and found the guiding words: "Take nothing with you on the road."

The third time he consulted the Scripture, he had the response: "If anyone wishes to follow me, let him deny himself, take up his cross and follow me."

"Brothers," cried Francis, "this is the life and rule for us and all who may want to join our company. Go, therefore, and comply with what you have heard."

A FIRE STARTED

The three men went to the plaza in front of St. George's. There Bernard distributed his property. It was an exhilarating and hilarious delight to give away handfuls of coin. Pressing in upon the crowd of beggers was a priest named Sylvester. He claimed he was underpaid, or not paid at all, for some stones

he had given Francis while San Damiano was being reconstructed. Francis dug deep into Bernard's purse and loaded the greedy priest with more than payment, asking at the same time, "Are you paid in full now?"

Back home, Sylvester was ashamed of himself. Soon, he too joined Francis. Peter Cattani likewise got rid of his possessions and asked Francis to take him as a friar.

Angelo Tancredi, when Francis found him was a knight of position and wealth, and with the enthusiasm that was always responsive to a challenge. Francis chaffed him at once: "Don't you think," he said, "that you have worn that belt and sword, and those fine spurs long enough? What about changing the belt for this rope, the sword for the Cross, and the spurs for the dust and stones of the road?" Angelo did just that, and Francis kept him close to himself.

Then came Leo, "the Pecorello" or "little Lamb of God," the exquisite penman, as the breviaries he made for Francis and Clare show to our wondering admiration; the secretary of the Saint and his advisor and confessor.

Another was Pacifico, once William of Lisciano, the King of Verses, who had been brought as a youth by an Emperor to the gay court of Palermo; had bandied ballads, love-songs, sonnets in contest with Norman and Provencal troubadours: had listened to fine-spun, courtly disquisitions, dialectics of learned Greeks and Arabs with their subtle learning: had taken part in Courts of Love and finally had been crowned laureate by the great Frederick himself. How Francis loved this songster!

Then Masseo, the tall, eloquent and comely man whom Francis ordered to be doorkeeper, almoner and cook, to teach him that obedience is sister of humility. Francis liked to banter with him and often took him along on trips.

Juniper, too, the literalist. For his literalism Francis said, "I wish I had a whole forest of such junipers!" Rufinus, the shy mystic, beset with doubts and fears until taught trust and love by Francis.

Giles, the ploughboy who had cast himself at Francis feet in the woods near the Portiuncula and begged to be taken into the order. He was the industrious Jack-of-all-trades, the shrewdest, wittiest, whose trenchant sayings have come down to us.

And Brother John the Simple who copied Francis without pausing or questioning. The peasant left his plow standing in the field when Francis came along; his heritage, an ox, he left to his relatives, followed Francis, and thereafter repeated Francis' every gesture and action. Even the saint could bear it no longer. Said John, "I have made the promise to do what you do. It would not be safe for me not to do it." Pleased, Francis cited Brother John as a model pupil and called him "Saint" John when the young man died an early death!

In that way the fire spread. Near St. Mary's of the Angels the penitents built themselves a hut of wattles and clay. The company grew; merchant, knight, priest, poet, ploughboy, canonist, simpleton —until they were twelve. Something had to be done.

TO MOTHER CHURCH

"Brothers," said Francis when the group numbered twelve, "I see that the Lord in his mercy means to increase our company. So, let us go to our mother, the holy Roman Church, and make known to the Pope what the Lord has begun to do through us so that we may carry on with what we have begun, with his pleasure and command" *Words,* no. 44. And to the very end Francis stood solidly, even vehemently on the authority of the Holy See.

From Innocent III in 1209 they obtained verbal approbation of their rule and permission to preach repentance. The rule consisted of a few extracts from the Gospels, but Francis regarded the whole Gospel as his rule of life.

At the beginning of the rule we find the four Gospel texts which constitute the basis of unconditional following of Christ, expressed in the words: "The rule of life for these brothers is that they live in obedience, in chastity, and without property and thus follow the teaching and example of our Lord Jesus Christ, who says (Mt. 19, 21): 'If you wish to be perfect, go, sell all you have and give it to the poor, and you will have treasures in Heaven; and come follow me.'"

And (Mt. 16, 24): "Whoever wishes to follow me, let him deny himself and take up his cross and follow me."

Likewise (Lk. 14, 26): "If anyone wishes to come to me and does not hate father and mother and spouse and children and brothers and sisters, yes, his very soul, he cannot be my disciple."

Finally (Mt. 19, 29): "And everyone who has left father or mother, brothers or sisters, spouse or children, home and land for my sake, shall have a hundredfold and possess eternal life."

How often these words have fallen on deaf or accustomed ears. Francis heard them with a freshness and urgency that demanded fulfillment at once. With perfect humility and utter simplicity he set about his task of living the Gospel of Christ. To know Christ meant for Francis reliving the life of Christ in every detail. The essence of knowing the Gospels meant their factual realization in his own life.

THE FIRST FRIARY

Back in Assisi the friars huddled together in a little hut in a hamlet outside of Assisi called Rivo Torto. It was near a leper settlement. So cramped were the quarters that Francis designated each friar's space by writing his name on the rafter above! They led a community life, worked where they could as hired hands, and brought the faith in the language of the people to the public squares of the mushrooming cities of Italy.

THE COMING OF ST. CLARE

Biographers of St. Clare have graphically portrayed the midnight scene of the eighteen-year-old girl fleeing from her father's house and flinging herself foolhardily at Francis' feet in the little chapel of

Portiuncula outside the walls of Assisi on the midnight of March 18, 1212.

Francis accepted her vows, sheared off her golden tresses and gave her a rough habit in exchange for the silken garments; a black veil to cover her shorn head.

Born July 16, 1194, Clare was twelve years younger than Francis. She came from a noble and wealthy family of influence. Surrounded by her family, admiring friends and suitors, with willing servants and the security of wealth in an unsteady, shifting age, she was probably envied by the ordinary girls of Assisi, and no doubt admired too, as the youth of Assisi admired Francis.

While Clare was growing up in girlhood, Francis was struggling for spiritual maturity and manhood. No doubt she often heard of him, probably often saw him, for Assisi is no different than any other small community where everyone, proverbially, knows everyone else's business. Besides, they both moved in the same social stratum. Francis was the talk of Assisi, and the bold, dramatic incidents of his life were enough to fire the imagination of this determined, sensitive, restless girl.

Here, Clare thought, was no wearing of a hair-shirt under a silk robe, no giving away of the crumbs from a rich table — but absolutely a following of Christ's command to forsake all and follow him. In the roughest peasant garb, Francis at the time was nursing lepers in the wretched huts on the plain below Assisi. With his early companions he was living near the Portiuncula, now given to the friars by the Benedictines of Mt. Subasio. Clare had watched the group grow. Already two of her cousins were with Francis—Rufino and the priest Sylvester. They had caused considerable talk in the relationship. Sorting the pros and cons, Clare at last was convinced of what she must do.

THE DRAMATIC EXIT

How could Clare ever hope to follow Francis in the kind of life he was living? Impossible to put her in the position of a modern girl in the United States who can, to a large extent, determine her own future. Her future was not hers to chose. At eighteen she was marriagable and was being pressed by suitors and by family.

Hearing a little barefoot friar eagerly preaching poverty, she caught a glimpse of her ideal of absolute renouncement, and determined to break with all her world in order to attain it. Her life's adventure was a ringing challenge to the sensuous spirit of her age.

Though actually little more than a child she acted with decision. In the Lent of 1212 Francis was preaching the sermons in the church of San Giorgio at Assisi. He had been invited to give the most important sermons of the year. Clare attended the sermons and wept, but not with the passive emotion of relief. It was the intense emotion that comes with decision.

Aided by her aunt Bianca Guelfucci, Clare had an audience with Francis and told him of her aspirations to leave all for Christ. He had no way of testing her sincerity except by the test he had given himself; dress in sackcloth and go begging for bread from door to door in Assisi! She did it, proving that she was of that persistent race that not only aspires but takes the kingdom of God by force. All through her life she showed that same calm courage and persistence. Never was she daunted or turned aside by trials.

The Lenten sermons were drawing to a close. Palm Sunday that year fell on March 18. Deep in the night of Palm Sunday Clare unbarred a secret door of the family mansion, hitherto blocked with beams and heavy stones. Without farewell she stepped out in the world of spiritual adventure. In Assisi they point out Clare's house and show you the door from which she fled.

In ancient Umbrian houses, special doors were made for the passage of bodies of those who died within. Living persons never used those doors.

Clare's using the so-called "Door of Death" to elope to the convent was a splendid piece of symbolism: dying to the world by leaving her father's mansion through the "Door of Death," seems like one of those dramatic actions characteristic of St. Francis himself.

THE NEW LIFE

Clare began her new life as Francis began his—by leaving home. And all her life she continued to be one of Francis' closest imitators. His "little plant" he called her. All his life Francis regarded Clare as the one who best understood what Christ had called him to: the perfect imitation of the Gospel life, especially that of total renunciation.

Always when he composed a poem, he wanted to send it to Clare. Once, when faced with a critical decision, he chose Clare out of all the world, to choose for him. When he was sick and dying, he turned to her to nurse him.

But on that night of March 18, 1212, Clare hurried with her aunt to the city gate, down the steep stony path to the plain, where the friars were reciting Matins at the Portiuncula. It was about an hour's hurried walk. Trembling and afraid, Clare came though the woods to the Portiuncula.

Drawing near, she saw that Francis had staged a welcome for her that she might be comforted and happy. All the friars were coming out in procession to meet Clare, carrying torches and candles and singing their gratitude to God. Bernard was there, and Peter and Giles, Leo, the little priest, and Angelo the knight of Rieti; and Sylvester and Rufino, Clare's cousins.

The peace and sweetness of the moment was immediately shattered by the shouts and sword Christ said he had come to bring, striking cleavage between a daughter and her father. Relatives tried to drag Clare back home; she clung to the altar and renewed her vows.

While the door was open waiting for Clare to come back, another sister, Agnes, rushed out to join Clare. Again, the fight to bring the sisters home. Again, a seemingly miraculous intervention by God which made Agnes so heavy even the muscled soldiers could not lift her.

The Poor Ladies, as Francis called them, now called the Poor Clares, the second order founded by Francis, first stayed with the Benedictine nuns. Later they had their own convent at San Damiano. Francis drew up a rule for them as simple as the one he made for the friars.

Clare had started a new youth movement for women of high spiritual adventure and the response was immediate and far-reaching. The sisters multiplied as fast as the brothers. From the ranks of the nobles of Europe, princesses and queens came to the Poor Ladies.

FRANCIS AND CLARE

Father and mother of the poor. Poverello and Poor Clare. Scorning the vulgarity of scratching for wealth and rank, and competing to be superior to others, Francis and Clare both achieved a new aristocracy of being equal with the lowest.

From the cloister of San Damiano, St. Clare spread her radiance throughout the world. Thomas of Celano tells us that in prayer shortly before Clare's birth, her mother Ortolana heard a voice saying to her, "Fear not, you will safely bring forth a light which shall light up all the world *clearly*." It was because of the last word of the prophecy that Clare received her name—a name of which we have no previous example, a personality of which we have no duplicate. Clara—a name and a personality which has had thousands of admirers and imitators these 700 years!

THE NEW ARISTOCRACY

The whole Franciscan movement appealed to the noblest and the best. The old aristocracy of blood and money was turned top side down; *the new aristocracy of Francis and Clare was to achieve the fine courtesy of being equal to the lowest.*

See what happened! His first disciples were Bernard of Quintavalle, a wealthy merchant, Peter Catani, a learned jurist, Angelo Tancredi, a knight, Leo and Sylvester, priests, Rufino, a son of the noble Scefi, and Clare, a daughter of the same noble house.

Presently his Third Order members joined his ranks: the Lady Giacoma Settesoli, a Roman patrician, Orlando, lord of Chiusi, John of Vellita, lord of Greccio, and the Lady Colomba, mistress of Monte Rainero.

After him came Louis, King of France; John, King of Jerusalem; Alton II, King of Armenia;

Roger Bacon, Dante, Giotto. Ciambue. And on down the centuries.

Clare, though never leaving San Damiano, counted among her followers, besides her own aristocratic family, Agnes, daughter of the King of Bohemia; Elizabeth, daughter of the King of Hungary, and another Elizabeth, Queen of Portugal and daughter of the King of England. Francis and Clare created a new and noble aristocracy across the world!

THE GREAT REFORM

As the number of friars grew their preaching activities increased. People began to "do penance," changed their lives radically. These great hosts of men and women in the world began clamoring in groups and as individuals for some program to stabilize their good intentions. They wanted to continue to shape their life and sentiments according to the spirit which they revered in Francis.

Francis seems to have complied with such demands as occasion offered. Out of these efforts to give people in the world a rule conformable to that of the friars and the Poor Ladies, grew at length the mighty movement known as the Third Order of St. Francis, or the Brothers and Sisters of Penance. The movement seems to have assumed a definite form, after the year 1221, although mention is made of a simple tertiary rule about 1209. (Celano, part 1, Chapter 15.)

The Third Order was thus merely an expansion of the idea of St. Francis. It had the same purpose in view and followed the same general spirit and regulations as the convent orders of St. Francis, and so, as St. Francis himself. Actually, it was a religious order for people living in the world. Since it was impossible for all the world to enter the convent, the convent and its life was brought out into the world and set to work in the home, in business, in all the various relations of man to man, and man to God.

Parents at home, husband and wife, merchant and peasant, master and servant, were to remain at their post, but all were to practice in their place the same spirit of detachment from the world, of self-denial and penance, of loyalty to the brotherhood and its activities, which the religious of the cloister practice by the vows of poverty, chastity and obedience.

The idea in this form was something new to the world. There had indeed been secular people attached to cloisters and following rules of daily life, but never had the goal of Christian perfection itself, fortified by a special rule, been proposed to them as their aim in life.

THE FIRST TERTIARIES

Credited as being the first members of the Third Order were Blessed Luchesio or Lucius, and his wife Buonadonna. Luchesio had been a politician and a merchant — some would have it, a business acquaintance of St. Francis' own family, and at one time quite as avaricious as old Peter Bernardone himself.

When the sensation created by the life of St. Francis began to make itself felt beyond the bounds of Umbria, in neighboring Tuscany, Luchesio was living at Poggibònsi, near Florence, retired from business and politics, and enjoying the luxury of early retirement. He seems to have been caught immediately by the spirit of the new movement, though his wife's sentiments were at first far from coinciding with those of her husband.

But the patience of Luchesio overcame the objections of Buonadonna, and so we see them both receiving the habit of the new order of the Brothers and Sisters of Penance in 1221, when the rule of this Third Order of St. Francis was approved by Pope Honorius III.

The rule itself seems to have been drawn up with the advice of Cardinal Ugolino, the life long friend of Francis, who succeeded Honorius III as Pope Gregory IX. The rule was modeled on that of other penitent societies of the day, but it was made to embody the essential spirit of the cloistral life.

The spirit which animated the early tertiaries has been the heritage of the Third Order ever since —a spirit of detachment from the world, of moderation, and penance, of charitable service under spiritual guidance.

It is a simple rule which everybody can understand. It lays no heavy burden on anybody, adapts itself to the weakest energies if only one has good will. Yet it soon has its earnest followers treading unimagined walks of virtue.

In the lives of those who have experienced a great spiritual change, the ideals of their earlier days frequently reappear under another guise in their later developments. The impetuous zeal shown by Saul the Pharisee advocating what he believed to be the truth, is an anticipation of Paul's apostolic enthusiasm in the cause of Christ. Our Lord recognized this law when he told the fisherman sons of Zebedee that they should become "fishers of men."

When St. Francis gave up the idea of donning armor, he did not abandon the hope of undertaking chivalrous adventure. The ideal of the Crusader still remained with him.

Those vast expeditions which Christendom sent forth during the Middle Ages against the Saracen had drained the manhood of Europe. They had been organized at first in response to the preaching of Peter the Hermit, reinforced by the authority of Pope Urban II, and had been entered upon with genuine religious enthusiasm.

The high resolves often degenerated and were dissipated in the jealousies and even open licentiousness in the crusading camps.

Francis resolved to go to the heart of the matter —to convert the infidel! But tempests cast the ship which was to take him to the Holy Land, on the coast of Slavonia, and he returned to Italy by way of Ancona. Soon after he tried to reach Morocco. But in Spain a severe illness sent him back.

Finally, in 1217, accompanied by Brother Illuminato, he begged passage from Ancona to St. John D'Acre on the coast of Syria and from there set out to Damietta, the infidel headquarters, where he determined to seek an audience with the Sultan Malekel-Kamel of Egypt. There was a price on Christian heads, he was warned Nonetheless he approached the Saracen sentinels and gained passage to the Sultan.

In the interview which he secured with Malek-el Kamel, Francis bore himself with such meekness and humility, and at the same time with such daring, that the Sultan not only did not suffer any harm to come to him but listened willingly to his words.

Francis begged the Sultan to light a mighty fire, declaring himself ready to mount it as a witness to Christ. But the infidel leader declined the test.

Though unsuccessful. Francis proved himself a true crusader, having transformed the sword into a pastoral staff. Not nineteen years after his death his friars would be marching across the steppes of Asia to bring the Gospel even to the Great Khan the Mongol—such was the crusading spirit he engendered in his order.

It is said that Francis obtained a perpetual permission from the Sultan for the friars to come and go, to beg and preach, without molestation. At any rate he did receive leave to visit Jerusalem and the Holy Places. And to this day the Franciscans are the custodians of the Holy Places of Palestine.

CHRISTMAS AT GRECCIO

Back in Italy in the fall of 1223, Francis set himself the task of drawing up a final Rule of the Order which was approved by Pope Honorius III on November 29, 1223. Relieved that the task was over, Francis' gaze went to the Holy Land. He saw the crib at Bethlehem again and he resolved to make the birth of Christ come alive before his very eyes.

Hastily he dispatched a note to wealthy friend, John of Vellita, asking him for the use of the grotto of Greccio for Christmas. Francis gave precise instructions. "For I want to observe the memory of the Child who was born at Bethlehem, and in some way see before my bodily eyes the discomforts of his baby needs, how he was laid there in a manger, and how, with the ox and the ass standing by, he was placed there on the hay."

The friars about Greccio were invited and the people of the countryside. They came that Christmas eve, winding up the steep mountain slopes with burning torches. The crib was ready: the hay, the ox and the ass.

"Solemn Mass was celebrated over the crib," so the account of Celano goes, "and the priest experienced a new kind of consolation,"

Francis, not a priest but a deacon, preached. Beside himself with sheerest delight, he stooped to behold the crib and we are told an infant seemed to come to life for a moment in his arms.

Here was Bethlehem again. At midnight. Out in God's nature. Among plain country folk. No vast church and expensive outlay. And above all, no irreverence. Pope Honorius' permission had been obtained in Rome. Not even Mary and Joseph were represented, so far as the accounts tell us. Much less the Divine Child. Just that vacant crib, which spoke volumes. Maybe that too was one of the things St. Francis was busy about in Rome: to see just how the original crib preserved in St. Mary Major's was made, so it could be exactly duplicated with its "five slender boards."

The words of the account insist that the crib was so placed that it acted as a kind of altar stone, or rather held the altar stone, and the Mass was said over it, so that at the moment of the Consecration Jesus really rested in St. Francis' little crib.

Once again, and more tellingly than any of the elaborate old representations could have done it, the undisguised lesson of the Faith was brought home to these country folk: the Christ of Bethlehem and the Christ of the Holy Mass and Eucharist are the same Christ offering himself for the welfare of the souls of men, loving every soul to the extreme and begging every soul to love him in return, thus illustrating Francis' words quoted in connection with his veneration of the Christmas story: "After the Lord was born for us, we just had to be saved" (... *oportuit nos salvari*, in the sense of "Shame on us if we did not save ourselves!").

In that sense Francis is the originator of our Crib devotion, which has become a standard part of our Christmas celebration in church and home, much as the Stations of the Cross are a year-round fixture of Catholic churches "introduced" by a Franciscan preacher of a later century, St. Leonard of Port Maurice.

Francis' Crib devotion is a symbol of all his life's work in that way—another instance where the initial words of the Church's prayer honoring St. Francis apply: "O Lord Jesus Christ, who with the world growing cold, in order to inflame our hearts with the fire of your love . . . gave us blessed Francis..."

For of course the Greccio idea caught on. It was realized that it need not be confined to the fastness of Greccio; that it has its place in churches and homes too, with due modification. The simple, simplified Crib became a feature of Franciscan Christmas celebrations everywhere, and happily it was copied everywhere.

49

It was a simple means Francis used. It was not planned elaborately. But it was done deliberately. Little did he think that tiny incident would become a tradition, intensifying with the passage of the centuries!

ON MT. LA VERNA

The ideals of chivalry always attracted Francis. St. Michael, the Archangel, was the patron of the medieval knights; he was the leader of the heavenly hosts and the sworn enemy of Satan. Along the Rhine and southern Germany, isolated mountains, formerly sacred to Wotan, were at this period dedicated to St. Michael. So too, in Cornwall and in Normandy, and all along the coasts of Sicily and Apulia, shrines or chapels dedicated to St. Michael were built.

When the Mount of LaVerna was given to St. Francis to use as a retreat by the great knight Orlando of Chuisi, it was characteristic of St. Francis to dedicate this outstanding peak at the head of the valley of the Tiber by some special act of honor to St. Michael. He resolved to keep a forty days-fast in preparation for the feast of St. Michael by spending it in prayer on LaVerna.

With his best loved brethren, Leo, Masseo. Angelo and Illuminato, the long fast began in August 1224. On a narrow ledge of rock above the cliffs Francis went on alone to spend the time in prayer and meditation. The gist of his long prayers have come down to us:

"O Lord Jesus Christ, I entreat you to give me two graces before I die: first, that in my lifetime I may feel in body and soul as far as possible the pain you endured, dear Lord, in the hour of your most bitter suffering; and second, that I may feel in my heart as far as possible that excess of love by which you, O Son of God, were inflamed to undertake so cruel a suffering for us sinners."

While Francis prayed, the friars waited in anticipation as though they had a premonition of something stupendous about to happen. On September 14, at the climax of a storm Francis was visited by the apparition of "a man bearing the likeness of a crucified Seraph." In that instant the marks of nails began to appear upon his hands and feet and a deep bleeding wound to open his side. The miracle was one which Francis kept hidden and which he asked his friars to keep secret, but slowly the rumor of this tremendous secret spread about the world.

No miracle of history has more testimony of external witness than this strange mystical manifestation. These marks, called the Stigmata, were seen by tens of thousands of people. Francis kept them covered while alive, but after his death they were seen and kissed by crowds of men and women, sceptics as well as believers, who came to the Portiuncula not only to venerate but to examine them. These marks were the consequence and the crowning proof of Francis' complete resemblance to Christ. Dante calls it the final seal upon the Rule, the sign of Christ's acceptance of what Pope Innocent had first approved and Honorius confirmed.

The Cross had triumphed in Francis on the feast of the Exaltation of the Cross, and now the Cross was to extend its arms over all creation in his person — over the hearts and minds of generation after generation and tens of thousands of followers century after century!

GOD'S GLORY THE EARTH PROCLAIMS

St. Francis loved nature like our Lord Jesus Christ. Our Lord exclaimed over the wayside lily because the love of the heavenly Father clothed it with more splendor than Solomon in all his glory. The rubbish - hunting ravens and the vagabond sparrows are object lessons of God's solicitous love of his creatures: they neither sow nor reap nor gather into barns, and "yet your heavenly Father feeds them."

St. Francis did not love nature merely because it pleased him; he hugged all nature to himself because it so marvelously praised God. He did not croon about nature like a sophisticated modern who thinks that it is the proper thing to do. Francis sang like the Psalmist, because he could hardly help chanting, "God's glory the heavens proclaim, his handiwork the heavens foretell" (Ps. 8).

GOD THE FATHER OF ALL

Since all creation tumbled from the touch of God's hand, everything was as close to St. Francis as a brother or sister. He felt a kinship to creation, as

fellow townsmen meeting by chance in a strange land are immediately on fraternal terms on discovering their common origin. Do not, by the way, leave with the idea that St. Francis was fond of animals. He was fond of creatures. Anyone can be fond of animals because they remind one of human beings. People can become quite sloppy about their fondness too. But only a child can sit and talk to a teddy bear for hours.

St. Francis was like that. He talked to the birds and bears and bees and crawling things, not because they reminded him of human beings, but because they revealed to him God's love and goodness. He was always acutely aware that he was a creature with creatures—a bird of a feather. He sang his Divine Office with the Larks. He realized his responsibility for creatures; he was tenderly anxious to protect them, concerned to ward off harm from them. The ugliest and most despised things were the closest to his heart, just as a mother loves her most backward and least handsome child the best.

His early biographer, Thomas of Celano, writes: "Every creature was a brother, and in an unusual way unknown to others did his profound sight pierce to the very depth of each creature as if he had already taken possession of the glorious freedom of the children of God." What he perceived was the utter dependence of all creation on the heavenly Father. For Francis all the universe was divided into different natural or religious orders, similar to his own but owing direct obedience to God, like the members of his own order. Everything, therefore, belonged to some order and was Brother or Sister.

For a man of the thirteenth century this concept would come easier than to us today. All society was divided according to vocations, trades and callings, and they followed the rules and restrictions of their orders and their guilds, trades or the allegiances they owed to a feudal lord.

As a young man Francis aspired to rise above the merchant status to the order of knighthood. He dreamed of becoming a famous knight with his own castle and vassals. By his complete renunciation his only liege lord to whom he belonged was his Creator. The Son of God, however, as Francis explains it, asked the heavenly Father for a new and humble people who would be unlike all others who have gone before and "would be content to have Christ only." These people constituted a new Order —a new people, his Friars Minor.

So he dealt with creatures as in "orders" and he approached them according to their own "Obedience" and their "Rules."

Thus we must understand his sermon to the birds. It was not so much for their instruction, but for his own.

THE SERMON TO THE BIRDS

On the road from Cannara (where the whole town wanted to follow Francis) to Bevagna the incident occurred which is so commonly associated with St. Francis in popular fancy. In an exuberance of feeling, we might pun that Francis did it for a lark. Better, he preached it for us. The *Fioretti* gives the substance of that famous sermon:

"My little sisters the birds, you owe much to God, your Creator, and you ought to sing his praise at all times and in all places, because he has given you liberty to fly about into all places; and though you neither spin nor sow, he has given you a twofold and a threefold clothing for yourselves and for your offspring. Two of all your species he sent into the Ark with Noah that you might not be lost to the world; besides which he feeds you, though you neither sow nor reap. He has given you fountains and rivers to quench your thirst, mountains and valleys in which to take refuge, and trees in which to build your nests; so that your Creator loves you much, having thus favored you with such bounties. Beware, my little sisters, of the sin of ingratitude, and study always to give praise to God." As he said these words, all the birds began to open their wings, and reverently to bow their heads to the ground, endeavoring by their motions and by their songs to manifest their joy to St. Francis. and the saint rejoiced with them . . . Having finished his sermon, St. Francis made the sign of the cross, and gave them leave to fly away. Then all the birds rose up into the air, singing most sweetly; and, following the sign of the cross, which St. Francis had made, they divided themselves into four companies.

They flew to the north, east, south and west "signifying thereby, that as St. Francis, the bearer of the Cross of Christ, had preached to them and made upon them the sign of the Cross . . . so the preaching of the Cross of Christ, renewed by St. Francis, would be carried by him and by his brethren over all the world, and that the humble friars, like little birds, should possess nothing in this world but should cast all the care of their lives on the providence of God."

Returning from the East a few years later, Francis and his companions came upon a flock of singing birds while crossing the Venetian marshes. At Francis' suggestion, the brothers said their breviary while the birds praised the Creator. But soon the lusty voices of the birds drowned out the friars. Francis chided: "My sisters, cease from singing until we have rendered our due praises to the Lord.

At another time while Francis was preaching at Aviano he could hardly be heard above the shrill twittering of the swallows. "My sisters the swallows," he cried, "it is now time that I should speak. Pray you keep silence until my preaching is ended."

A similar episode took place at the Carceri, a favorite mountain retreat of St. Francis; at another time a benediction of many birds. At LaVerna where he received the Stigmata, the birds came to him freely and especially a certain falcon that would not leave him. At Siena it is a pheasant; at the Portiuncula a cicada; at Greccio a leveret; on the island in Lake Trasimene, a rabbit; at the lake of Rieti, a waterfowl; at another time near Siena, a flock of sheep. But most famous and most strange of all is the tale of the Wolf of Gubbio.

THE WOLF OF GUBBIO

The story hardly needs telling, so well known is it. Gubbio was afflicted by a plague—a wolf, perhaps a pack of wolves. Attempts to rationalize this story to make out that this "Wolf" was a fierce robber by the nickname of "Wolf" do not seem to have foundation.

The simple facts are that the citizens of Gubbio were scared. The wolf had raided again and again. Attempts to capture him had failed. Obviously St. Francis' power over animals had spread abroad. So when he came to Gubbio it was natural for the citizens to beseech Francis to tame the wolf.

In a solitary place outside the town, Francis met and tamed a wolf. "Come here brother wolf; I command you, in the name of Christ, neither to harm me nor anybody else." The *Fioretti* says that the wolf "coming up to St. Francis, lay down at his feet as meekly as a lamb." St. Francis made an agreement with the wolf: shelter and food from the citizens of Gubbio if he would be a good wolf. Brother wolf agreed by nods and signs. Continues the *Fioretti*: "The wolf lived two years at Gubbio; he went familiarly from door to door without harming anyone, and all the people received him courteously, feeding him with great pleasure, and no dog barked at him as he went about. At last, after two years, he died of old age, and the people of Gubbio mourned his loss greatly; for when they saw him going about so gently among them all, he reminded them of the virtue and sanctity of St. Francis."

This seemingly natural quality in St. Francis to draw animals and to subject them, has supernatural implications as he himself intimates. Being perfectly obedient to God himself, he sums up creation's obedience to its master. Just as a dog will not obey a master who has no control over himself, so Francis being perfectly obedient to God was recognized by creatures as their perfect master. "All things are yours, and you are Christ's and Christ is God's."

In Francis' "Salutation of the Virtues", probably composed at LaVerna in 1216, he gives us the clue when he addressed "Holy Obedience."

> "Holy obedience shames all self-will of flesh and body, and keeps a body mortified to obey the spirit, and obey one's fellow man. It makes a person *subject to anybody in the world; and not to men alone, but to all the beasts and wild things*, so that they can do what they please with him so far as the Lord on high might grant it them" *Words*, no. 68.

The essence, or distinguishing element of every category of creation was the submission of its "carnal will" in holy obedience to its Creator. Obedience was not only to free the soul from fear, from anger and from wordly care, but to enable a Brother, being as a "dead body in the hand of his superior," to draw on infinite strength from his dependence. This great Franciscan virtue is the fount of power, the source of peace, the well-spring of miracle, and the key to the Rule of the mystic order in the natural world by which St. Francis subjected all things to himself!

THE CANTICLE OF BROTHER SUN

Francis finished his fast on LaVerna and had to be carried down on an ass led by Brother Leo. A peasant met him and asked in rustic simplicity if he were the Brother Francis everyone talked so much about. Assured that he was, the rustic said to the mystic: "Let me give you some advice! Be sure you are what people think you are otherwise there will be a lot of disappointed people!" For that Francis kissed the man's feet.

Back at the Portiuncula, the old flair for far-flung preaching took hold of him again in early summer of 1225. The friars remonstrated. Finally Cardinal

Ugolino urged Francis to come to Rieti to the bishop's palace so that he could be given the proper care.

But he only got as far as San Damiano — ten minutes from the Portiuncula. There Clare insisted that he stay until he became stronger. A little hut was made for him in the garden of San Damiano. In the hut the Saint's eyes pained him so badly that he could endure neither the sunlight nor the gleam of fire. He cried for help to bear the ailment patiently. Then came the joyous tidings like the burst of Bethlehem's Gloria: "Sing amid your illness and infirmity, for the kingdom of Heaven is already yours!"

Now Francis was flooded with the overwhelming understanding of God's blessings. From his heart welled forth that great hymn to the Lord of creation amid his creature world. Suffering had released the song. The whole creature world, he said, must "serve the Lord in great humility." And to him humility and obedience were like twin sisters.

And the secret of the song was that it raised the whole creature world up to God in praise—the world that brings both pain and joy: Brother Sun in whom St. Francis once delighted but which now was painful to his eyes. All was accepted because all were obedient to what God wanted of them and "served the Lord in great humility."

Most high, almighty, and good Lord,
Yours is the praise, the glory, honor, blessing
all.

To you, Most High, alone of right they do
belong,
And no mortal man is fit to mention you.

Be praised, my Lord, of all your creature world,
And first of all Sir Brother Sun,
Who brings the day, and light you give to us
through him,
And beautiful is he, agleam with mighty
splendor:

Of you, Most High, he gives us indication.

Be praised, my Lord, through Sisters Moon
and Stars:
In the heavens you formed them,
bright and fair and precious.

Be praised, my Lord, through Brother Wind
Through Air, and cloudy, clear and every kind
of Weather
By whom you give your creatures sustenance.

Be praised, my Lord, through Sister Water,
For greatly useful, lowly, precious, chaste is she.

Be praised, My Lord, through Brother Fire,
Through whom you brighten up the night,
And fair he is, and gay, and vigorous, and
strong.

> Be praised, O Lord, through our sister Mother
>   Earth,
> For she sustains and guides our life,
> And yields us divers fruits, with tinted flowers,
>   and grass.
>
> Praise and bless my Lord, and thank him too.
> And serve him all, in great humility.

After he had composed the words, he no doubt consulted Brother Pacifico for the tune, for Pacifico had once been crowned "King of Verse" by the Emperor Henry IV. Then Francis sent his friars out into the world to sing the Canticle in the marketplaces, just as any well-known poet of Provence would send "jongleurs" to sing his songs in honor of his lady. "We are the minstrels to the Lord," he told them, "and what else are the servants of God but his minstrels, whose work it is to lift up people's hearts and move them to spiritual gladness" *Words* no. 271.

When Francis lay dying, a quarrel broke out between the bishop and the podesta (mayor) of Assisi: the bishop excommunicated the podesta and the podesta boycotted the bishop. Francis composed another verse to his canticle of Brother Sun and told some of his friars to bring the two enemies together and to sing to them:

> "Be praised, my Lord, through those who
>   pardon give for love of you,
> And bear infirmity and tribulation:
>
> Blessed are they who suffer it in peace,
> For of you, Most High, they shall be crowned."

The bishop and the podesta listened and were immediately moved. Both confessed themselves to be in the wrong, begged forgiveness, and came to terms. There was no attempt to weigh the pros and cons, rights and wrongs. Francis had created an atmosphere of love that is a solvent for the petty quarrels of life.

Through all his trials and sufferings, Francis returned to his earliest aspiration, the exhilarating concept of being God's troubadour, converting the world to love, penance, peace, and joy!

THE LAST DAYS OF ST. FRANCIS

At length, in early September, the friars carried Francis by easy stages to Rieti. His entrance into Rieti, riding on an ass, was a triumphal progress. The whole town, from magistrate and bishop to beggar turned out to meet him. The cripples and diseased, the blind and maimed were brought to him to be healed by the sign of the Cross that he made over them.

Hardly was he lodged in the bishop's house than his longing for solitude drove him to the little hermitage of Fonte Colombo where three years earlier he had written the Rule. Though his pains and infirmities were many, the agony in his eyes became almost intolerable. The doctor thought it best to resort to the medieval remedy of the cautery and the red hot iron was prepared.

"O Brother Fire," cried St. Francis, "you are among all creatures most noble and useful, be courteous to me now; for I have ever loved you for love of your Creator." The doctor was amazed for Francis bore the pain without a whimper — pain, which the doctor said, he feared to inflict on the strongest man. It seems the same thing was done again later.

Still burning to spread the kingdom of God, he summoned up the courage of his friars by encouraging: "My brothers, let us begin to serve God better; for all we have done so far is nothing!"

Counselled by Cardinal Hugolino to take Francis to a physician in Siena, Brother Elias, the minister general, had the Saint transported there. But no avail. A violent hemorrhage warned of the end. Elias immediately took him to the Celle of Cortona, a beautiful hermitage, where Francis rested for a month.

Brother Elias was bent on getting Francis back to Assisi so that he could die in his native town. To avoid Perugia, whose inhabitants wanted to claim Francis, Elias and his little band had the ailing Saint carried from Cortona over the difficult mountain pathways to Gubbio and on to Gualdo and Nocera. From there, east to Assisi through the little township of Satriano. At Nocera a band of knights and citizens of Assisi met them (so precious was the burden) to escort them to Assisi by the gorge of the torrent Tescio.

Arrived at Assisi, the dying man was lodged in the episcopal palace where eighteen years ago he had made his supreme renunciation. Citizens crowded around the palace day and night; a guard was placed over Francis. Francis sang and some of the friars rushed to shush him fearing that the more sober citizens might be scandalized because he was taking death so lightly! Angels sang and played for him instead!

At Assisi, or perhaps earlier at the Celle of Cortona, Francis dictated his Testament, leaving to all times the legacy of his spiritual outlook.

When Doctor Buongiovanni was called in at Siena back in mid-July, Francis asked him frankly how long he had. The doctor confessed that Francis would not outlive the autum. With a cheer the Saint flung up his arms, "Welcome, Brother Death!"

He sang his Canticle of Brother Sun again, and added his last verse:

> 'Be praised, my Lord, through our Brother Death of Body,
> From whom no man among the living can escape.
>
> Woe to those who in mortal sins will die;
> Blessed those whom he will find in our most holy graces,
> For the second death will do no harm to them."

When the end was approaching, they carried him from the bishop's house to the Portiuncula down in the valley, outside the city gates. There he wanted to die and outside the gate he asked the litter-bearers to put him down and face him toward Assisi. On his beloved Assisi he invoked God's richest blessings. There followed the farewells to Sister Clare and to Lady Giacoma of Settesoli. To Brother Bernard, Brother Elias, to all the friars and finally to his physician.

He gave a few final instructions: "When you see that I am being brought toward the end, lay me naked on the floor as you found me three days ago, and let me lie there in death for as long a time as it takes to walk a mile leisurely" *Words* no. 277.

He dragged on until October 3. On his last day he blessed the brothers corporately and singly, laying his right hand on the head of Bernard his "beloved first-born." Then, a symbolist to the last, in imitation of Christ, he caused bread to be brought and broken for him, and the pieces he distributed to the friars one by one with a last commandment that they should love one another.

While one of the friars read the suffering of Christ according to St. John, the Little Poor Man, at his own request, was laid on the bare earth, and his head sprinkled with ashes. He wanted to die in the utmost poverty: naked, as the naked Christ died. God was indeed now his God and his all. He had nothing and no one else.

Once again he sang his Canticle of Brother Sun and then intoned the 141st Psalm: "I cried to you, O Lord, I said, you are my hope, my portion in the land of the living." He went right down "as well as he could" to the last verse, which came out loud and clear: "Bring my soul out of prison, that I may give thanks to your name." God released him from the narrow prison of his body, so that he could roam about in the spacious mansions of God's love. "The poor little body," Brother Elias wrote later to the provincial ministers, "seemed to shine with a transformed radiance and looking at the glowing wounds one could only think of the risen Christ."

Over the convent roof in the sunset skies gathered with joyous song a great multitude of larks heralding God's chosen singer into Paradise.

Around the Portiuncula during those last days friars and Assisians had gathered. Each one was feeling the loss personally. "Il Poverello" — the Little Poor Man's body belonged to Assisi and the citizens guarded it jealously. But Il Poverello is everybody's — everybody who has learned to see with his vision and to live with his spirit!

Water looks very simple until the chemistry professor draws a diagram of the chemical arrangement of oxygen and hydrogen in a molecule of water. Again, when he begins showing us by means of circles the molecular arrangement of sugar, the diagram becomes more complex — so many circles this way, so many that way, all romping about the blackboard. We have all pouted pensively, in studying the elements of the nuclear arrangement (call it that) of the atom bomb as described in popular journals. How the whole thing suddenly shifts with hurricane swiftness when the bomb explodes!

The life of St. Francis is a kind of atomic formula. We think we have his life captured and capsulized in sterilized little formulas. Suddenly a chain reaction sets in, a new view of Francis rearranges the whole formula with explosive suddenness. But the ingredients are the same.

When St. Francis spoke of Sister Water and Brother Fire, perhaps he was giving us a hint. Like water, he too was simple, yet complex. Like fire, his nature can no more be sharply outlined than a flame flickering and frolicking.

To define his personality is a difficult task. Just when his gentleness, courtesy, loyalty, poverty, love of the Crucified, joyousness, understanding, charming manner and kindness have captivated us, suddenly all these facts of Francis vanish into the single quality of simplicity. We have gathered up all the bold, heraldic colors that characterize him, and find them coming from the prism of his person as a single shaft of white light.

Nonetheless we can pick out three characteristics of St. Francis which are, with the grace of God, the foundation of the spirit of St. Francis. They are his childlike naturalness, his nobility and chivalry, and his energetic will as a leader.

HIS NATURALNESS

Francis was always himself — Brother Francis, "your little one and servant." He could never be deluded or duped into duplicity. If he must allow the friars to sew a piece of fur on the inside of his habit to keep him warm, the outside must have one too. If, in his weakened condition, the doctor gave him chicken broth during Lent, the people had to be told he was a glutton before he began preaching. If an uncharitable thought flitted through his mind, immediately Francis was on his knees begging pardon from his brothers. Of all men, no one could have been more sincerely honest with others and with himself.

Whether he stood before pope or peasant, he spoke and acted as Brother Francis, the friar minor. He preached as naturally to an audience of cardinals in the Vatican as he preached to the canaries in the valley. It seemed no bit more stange to him to speak to one group than before the other. One time, nervously anxious for Francis, Cardinal Hugolino persuaded the Saint to prepare carefully before addressing the cardinals. Francis did. But, like the Cure of Ars after him, preparation petrified his spontaneity. Francis asked the pope's blessing and began preaching without the slightest embarrassment. He was inspired. His hands and feet moved in rhythmic accompaniment. Cardinal Hugolino, huddled up in his great cloak, prayed fervently that the Holy Ghost might not desert his dear friend. Francis never gave it a thought whether the cardinals might jeer or applaud. He spoke what was closest to his heart.

Do not mistake the naturalness of St. Francis for the modern connotation of the word, now so closely synonymous with "uninhibited" — acting on the first best impulse. No, it is rather the uncalculating, guileless naturalness of a child that has not yet learned to take itself seriously. The naivete and naturalness of a child amuses us, because a child never bothers about futile questions. The bruised leg of the doll is kissed, no matter that the doll is not alive.

Had Francis cared to consider it, he would have agreed that even though he saved two sheep from slaughter by buying them with his cloak, two others would take their place at the slaughter house; even though he put the pike back in the pond, it would probably be caught by another fisherman. Yet, like a child, he was not looking at the result of his action, but the deed itself. He considered results less important than the example set by his actions.

If there was a flaw in Francis, it was the delicate dissimulation taught by our Lord in the Gospel. It was a kind of holy hypocrisy, the very antithesis of duplicity. Francis employed all the art the hypocrite uses, not to attract praise, but to avoid it. Do not

parade for praise if you are fasting; wash your face; anoint your body, shut the door of your room and pray to your Father in secret — these recommendations pleased Francis so greatly that he incorporated the texts in his rule.

Bernard of Quintavalle, the first of Francis' followers, wanted to test him before joining him. He invited Francis to his house and placed a luxurious bed at his disposal. Francis seemed quite pleased and pretended to sleep. When at length he believed everyone had retired (Bernard was peeking from behind the curtains), Francis arose and passed the night in prayer.

Francis was always grateful for a reminder that he must never be anything but what he actually was. Coming down from Mt. LaVerna, wounded and weakened by the stigmata, a peasant approached and asked if he were the Francis everyone was talking about. Francis answered he was. The rustic then gave the mystic a sound piece of advice: "Be sure that you are everything people think you are, because many have their confidence in you." Francis reacted wholeheartedly, dismounted from the donkey and knelt to kiss the hand of the counselor.

THE MAN OF IDEALS

Everything in Francis was honest, true, manly. He was by nature noble and chivalrous. Both words are colorless today. Perhaps they can both be summarized in a single word — integrity. Integrity must mean fulness and completeness of personality and being — the *integer* being oneness or wholeness. It is the source of greatness, of sincerity, of responsibility, of honor. It is the root of those attributes which make leadership fruitful and faithful and effective.

It was no accident that Francis knew no higher ideal in his youth than knighthood. The ideal meant much more for him than military grandeur. In fact, we can hardly picture St. Francis finding any joy in a military career as such. The knight of Francis' dreams was the perfect man: noble, grand, good with the indefinable thing we call character. He must be joyously carefree and heroically courageous, but at the same time loyal, gentle, merciful, mild and pure-minded. All the powers of the knight must be consecrated to the good and the beautiful, but he must also have an understanding heart and a keen eye for the ugly, the small, the weak, and the needy.

Francis possessed many of these knightly qualities by nature. Though he spent lavishly on himself, he was ever open-hearted and magnanimous toward the poor. Celano says he exchanged the weapons of the flesh for those of the spirit, the wordly military fame for the Divine knighthood. Wonderful exchange! Now his whole ideal was to be Christ's most faithful knight. Much of his life was governed by this thought. He was ready to offer everything for the love of Him who called him to his service. Dangers and difficulties? They are but opportunities to prove his loyalty and show his gratitude. Discouraged by them? This was perfect joy in the Lord's service!

Above all the knight must have a heart. In all the severe privations Francis imposed on himself, he always allowed his heart the right to be joyful. He was not ashamed to possess a heart, nor did he fear to listen to the voice of the heart.

It showed itself especially in his merciful mildness with everyone. Being merciful is of its nature a chivalrous and romantic performance. It involves delay; we lose time; we must listen to long stories and in the end confess that we are unable to help. In a highly geared civilization such as ours, being merciful is an unpractical quality. In Francis' day he could take off his cowl and even his habit, to give it to the poor; he could even strip the altars if need be. If Francis' action can be explained, today it would probably be explained away.

Today, we are liable to read about the knightly exploits of Francis and assimilate them in our minds much in the same way we read about the Arabian Nights. We think of both as coming from the pages of poetry and romance. They are charming. There is the danger! There is no reason to go to poetry to explain Francis. He was real and consistently merciful because he had integrity — the wholeness and completeness of putting on Christ.

Francis was, above all, a true product of the age of chivalry. Courtesy was a basic quality of his nature. So highly did he value it that he thought of it as one of the attributes of God. He wanted his friars to be anything but rude. Since his time selfishness, ugliness and greed have found themselves steadily restrained by the chivalrous and subtle influence of St. Francis of Assisi.

•

THE LEADER

We dare not cloud over a third characteristic of St. Francis, namely, his energetic will. We are so apt to get the wrong impression: exterior mildness does not mean interior mulberriness. There was nothing soft nor slovenly in the intensity with which he held his will from wavering. He could not bear to hold a mere frozen idea before his mind. Immediately the thing had to be carried into action by effort of will.

He never dodged difficulties; they were mastered. Nothing could intimidate him; he never shirked once his mind had been made up. The intensity of his will made him a leader. Even as a youth he was elected the King of Youth. He must have had something to offer to be admitted even in the circles of the nobility of Assisi. He was an initiator, not an imitator. To the very end he faced new situations without reference to the past. When he sat down to write a rule for his men, he did not want the minutes of the last meeting; the rules of St. Benedict and St.

Bernard were not for his friars, he said. This was something new. It had to be carried through by wholehearted determination in following out the life of Friars Minor.

Because he stuck to his ideal so steadfastly, benedictions undreamed of sprang up after him. When he spoke his vows to Lady Poverty, he was initiating a movement he had never even guessed. He was not conscious of a social and economic order being affected by his determined adherence to poverty. The brothers were to live literally from hand to mouth. When Francis said God would provide for him, he was making no pious profession of his confidence in Divine Providence; he was announcing a solution.

Nothing could make him swerve from his course, not even the barbed remarks of his brothers. "You are neither beautiful, nor noble, nor learned. Why, then, does all the world follow you?" But neither did Francis have what we usually describe as an iron will synonymous with bullheadedness. No one could have been less dictatorial, less petty than he. He was ever ready to sacrifice the letter of the law if by so doing he could foster its spirit. Even when he describes the qualities of a "perfect general of the Order," Francis pictures a man that, far from insisting on all his authority, is always ready to make any reasonable concession if by so doing he may save a soul.

Still, Francis never dawdled, never delayed. He was like a child who goes out with a shovel to dig a hole for the sea; Francis was going out to bring all men to God. The unwitting audacity of his projects surprises us just because of the swift reliance between the thought and action taken.

Looking at the natural characteristics of St. Francis, we see a unique and charming harmony of opposites. He was simple and at once ingeniously natural. He was fired by enthusiastic ideals of the great and good and beautiful, but always stooped to the smallest and the ugliest of God's creatures. Depth and warmth of feeling were not extinguished by a persevering energy of will. Severe with himself, he was enduringly tender of heart towards others.

For all we have said, Brother Francis might be Brother Flame. In fact, he is something like a flame. Around the heart of a flame there is a faint iridescent nimbus so distinct that one never doubts that it can be seized. We have tried to seize that nimbus by putting down three natural characteristics of St. Francis which grace built on: his naturalness, his chivalry and his energetic will.

GOOD MORNING, GOOD PEOPLE

Near the Center of the village of Poggio Bustone in Italy there is a white stone in a wall with the inscription: "Buon Giorno, Buona Gente — Good Morning, Good People." This is the greeting St. Francis gave to the villagers as he entered Poggio Bustone in 1209, explains the inscription. To this day, on the feast of the saint, one of the villagers rises very early and goes from door to door with a tambourine tinkling. As he knocks at each door, he calls to the people within, "Buon giorno, buona gente,"

Good People! But it is said that the people of Poggio Bustone were a degenerate lot, lost in sin; they had begged St. Francis to stay with them to make them good. He came to the town with a bow that was almost like an obeisance. Obediently he came not to be served, but to serve. His smile smote their darkened faces; his greeting drove out of their hearts all hesitance and mistrust. "Good morning, good people!"

UNFAILING REVERENCE

Good People! There is the secret of his apostolate. The whole apostolate of Francis of Assisi proclaims his belief in the truth that you cannot really help or convert a man unless you first learn to love him. But you cannot love him unless you first believe in his fundamental goodness — unless you reverence him. His was an apostolate of reverence and respect for everybody. He saw in man the goodness that Christ loves and respects. In the soul of Francis all had become one immense wonder and reverence for Christ's gift of himself to every man. It was wonder and awe at so supreme a gift that Francis poured out upon all men.

"He honored all men," Chesterton says. "That is, he not only loved but respected them all. What gave him his extraordinary personal power was this: that from the pope to the beggar, from the sultan of Syria in his pavillion to the ragged robbers crawling out of the wood, there was never a man who looked into those brown burning eyes without being certain that Francis Bernardone was really interested in him, in his own inner individual life from the cradle to the grave; that he himself was being valued and taken seriously."

In all this there is no syrupy sentimentality. Those who reduce St. Francis to a poetic legend, speak as though Francis lived in an illusory world sparkling with newborn light lit by birds with strange sweet song, and gracious animals, and living whispering trees. But St. Francis by the grace of Christ saw Reality, not a poetic illusion. When he looked at mankind, he was not melted by modern slipshod aspirations towards fraternity, goodwill and brother-hood. He looked at men and women with the good tidings of the Gospel ringing in his ears.

THE DIVINE FAVOR

"Behold, I make all things new," the Lord says in the Apocalypse. No change in the substance of things was meant, but a change in the eyes of him who beholds the substance. St. Francis possessed those wonderfully changed and newly empowered eyes: they stripped each man down to the reality which Christ beheld. What he saw, found utterance in his dictum: "So much a man is, as he is in the sight of God, no more."

"Consider, O man," St. Francis wrote, "how is the excellence in which the Lord has placed you, because he has created and formed you to the image of his beloved Son according to the body, and to his own likeness according to the spirit." That is the reality which Francis beheld: the new creation. "If a man is in Christ, he is a new creature" (2 Cor. 5, 17).

God's love has raised man to a dizzy height: "Behold what manner of love the Father has bestowed on us, that we should be called children of God; and such we *are*" (1 John 3, 1). Since everyone is called to be or actually is a child of God, Francis can see nothing in anyone but his brother, whom he loves.

"But you are all brothers," he tells his friars. "And call no one your father on earth; for one is our Father, who is in Heaven." At the head of the great family of men stands God the Father. God created people in order to be their Father and to draw to himself all who wish to be his children. The home of all men is the happiness of Heaven. This is the good tidings which Jesus brought; that is the Gospel that rang in the ears of Francis as he looked at people.

He was amazingly oblivious to those distinctions of culture and class which are instinctive with us— save with children under the age of seven. Instinctively we look not at the inner soul of a person, but at his useful adjuncts: his money, his status, his education, his features, his clothes. But when St. Francis met a man or women, while being joyously aware of their individuality, he saw their substance, their basic reality in relation to God, Christ and himself.

"Every man must stand in awe of his own nature," Celano quotes St. Francis.

AN INSTRUMENT OF REFORM

In the hand of Francis, this reverence and respect proved a means of working reform in others. When certain villagers pointed accusing fingers at an unworthy priest, Francis hurriedly humbled himself in the dust before the priest and lifted the bewildered man's hand reverently to his lips: "I know not whether these hands are unclean or not . . . but these hands have touched my Lord . . . For himself, he may be bad; for me, he is good."

The priest's broken self-respect was restored, even while he was shamed into goodness. His authority among his parishioners was upheld by the most respected man in Italy. No invective could have worked more miraculously. Scorn and ridicule would only have eaten the cantankerous canker of disunity and ill-will deeper in the hearts of both priest and people. Francis opposed deaf ears to the accusations; he had a particular horror of calumny — a fault to which the masses are inclined.

Nothing could have been farther removed from the popular reaction than Francis' habit of venerating all priests indiscriminately because of the sacerdotal character of their office. "Wherever they might find priests, the friars were to bow their head before them and to kiss their hands; if they met them on horse back, Francis would even have them kiss not only their hands but the very hoofs of the horses on which they rode, out of respect for their office" (Three Companions).

When some friars had spoken contemptuously of a band of brigands, Francis rebuked the brothers, sent them out after the robbers, and bade them beg their pardon and invite them courteously to the convent. No doubt to the brigands' own embarrassment and perhaps, surprise, they were all converted and changed their lives. It was such a simple, gentle gesture, but it was genuine and soul-changing.

Again, there was the quarrelsome leper who was so impatient, unbearable and arrogant that everybody was sure he was possessed by the Devil. In the end the friars decided to abandon him to his own devices. Francis heard of it and promptly went to the leper, not to rebuke him or scold the already obdurate heart, but to greet him, as he says, "with balm-bearing words of gentleness." "God give you peace, my dearest brother." Through Francis' persistent patience not only the leprous skin, but the leprous soul was finally healed. Good people!

He never condoned irreverence or scorn. Gentleness was the touchstone. He told his friars: "Let all men be roused to peace, good-will and mercy through your gentleness. That is the very purpose of our calling that we way heal the wounded, bind up the broken-hearted, and recall those who have erred" (Three Companions). You cannot teach love by violence and cruelty; harshness and excessive severity, he told his brothers, only drive men farther from God.

Again and again he reminded the friars of "the benignity of Christ." Courtesy, he told them, was one of the Divine attributes. Anger in oneself and in others, he wrote in the rule of the First Order, hinders charity. The friars must be considerate of everyone but themselves: "I warn and admonish my friars not to despise or judge men whom they see clothed in soft and fine garments or eat and drink sumptuously, but rather let each one judge and despise himself" (Testament).

Good People! For him people were good because they were "good" for Christ. Read and reread his story, and you will find no hint that he marked the slightest difference, except in the secret folds of the soul, between the pope and the peasant, the bishop and the brigand, the learned lawyer, and the languid lady, the nobleman and the nobody. He spoke a universal language; he never sought to assume anyone's peculiar tone. He remained always the same. He was indeed the brother of fire, equally magnificent in the fire-place of the poor and of the rich. He was brother to the sun: it warms both the bad and the good. He was brother to Sister Water: it cleanses the filthy and refreshes the clean. In particular, Francis was oblivious of those petty distinctions of culture which count for so much with us.

In the first rule Francis demands of his friars: "And they ought to rejoice when they converse with lowly and despised persons, with the poor and weak, with the infirm and lepers, and with those who beg in the streets." He had an inherent liking, not so much for the poor as for those who had nothing at all: the rascals and the vagrants, the lepers and the absolute paupers. Toward them his courtesy was complete, his court manners exquisite, for they were to him the "heralds of the Great King." Though he could not always alleviate their wants, still he sought to console them. The frequent use of the word "consolation" in the Franciscan sources throws a light-house beam on those far-away beginnings. It pierces deep down, ferreting out what we have perhaps forgotten of the Franciscan spirit. You cannot console unless you reverence and believe sympathetically in a man's fundamental goodness.

Francis began by forcing himself to sympathize with people — not only a theoretical sympathy, as philosophers would say, "a notional assent" but a "real assent." Many good people display much good-heartedness, but waste energy on sentiment. Others — the few — show little sentiment, but brood for action. Francis brooded for action. He had long felt a sentimental sympathy for the lepers; but it took long hours of prayer and the grace of God to bring him to washing the wounds of lepers. Finally came the swift transfer of thought to action. "Thenceforth he began more and more to despise himself, until by the grace of God he had attained to perfect mastery over himself." Sentiment needs to be put in a harness. Sympathy is not weakening; it gives birth to humility and mastery.

WHERE TO START

We all incline to be sympathetic toward ourselves. We have to learn to be so toward others. We are not the only persons facing troubles and problems. Francis began by feeling sorry for almost everyone he met—the rich nobles, so deluded; poor peasants, chafing under their poverty. Often they cannot even put into words what rankles at the bottom of their hearts. Each individual has his own secrets, his own self within him. Probably, most likely a suffering self. He is so used to it that he does not even notice the pain. But right there in the midst of all the technique, the poise and the posing and the playing up to environment, you will most often find a dark and suffering self.

Now, is this sentimentality? Not at all. The gentle sympathy of St. Francis proves itself in going out to what we like least. St. Francis no more liked, felt fond of, or emoted over the leper he found on those Umbrian plains than we would have. He forced himself to do the Christian thing, and with that violence he carried off the kingdom of Heaven. Speaking of the incident in his last Testament, the Saint tells us: "And the Lord led me among lepers, and I showed mercy to them. And that which seemed bitter to me was turned for me into sweetness of soul and body."

"The worldly man," writes C. S. Lewis, "treats certain people kindly because he likes them. The Christian, trying to treat everyone kindly, finds himself liking more and more people as he goes on — including the people he could not even have imagined himself liking at the beginning."

In his dealing with people Francis clung to "one rag of luxury," the manners of the court. "But whereas in court there is one king and a hundred courtiers," writes Chesterton, "in this story there was one courtier moving among a hundred kings. For he treated the whole mob of men as a mob of kings." Throwing a coin to the downtrodden does not give the man back his broken self-respect. One gentle gesture will do it. "Through your gentleness . . . bind up the broken-hearted . . ." says Francis.

St. Francis moved among men with that gentle gesture: smiling, bowing, gesturing recognition from right to left, going down on the knees to his spirit to all with the reverent greeting, "Good morning, good people."

HERALD

BOOKS